# CATHERINE MALANDRINO

© 2008 Assouline Publishing
601 West 26th Street, 18th floor
New York, NY 10001, USA
Tel.: 212 989-6810   Fax: 212 647-0005
www.assouline.com

French translations by Nancy Dunham

Color separation by Luc Alexis Chasleries
Printed in China

ISBN: 978 2 75940 168 0

10  9  8  7  6  5  4  3  2  1

PASCALE RICHARD

# CATHERINE MALANDRINO

ASSOULINE

i t was the year 2001, and the French fashion designer Catherine Malandrino celebrated the new millennium by presenting her *Flag* collection in New York, draping her models in flowing dresses printed with the Stars-and-Stripes and cutting iconoclastic notched T-shirts from the U.S. flag. In doing so, she created a fashion show based on her American Dream— *Easy Rider* and vast spaces. She married two cultures: the couture of France and the casualness of America. Like Jasper Johns in his day, Catherine reinvented the starry banner in her own style. Her boldness seduced New York department store Bergdorf Goodman, which displayed the designs in its windows on Fifth Avenue.

A few months later, with the trauma of September 11, the *Flag* collection seemed premonitory. Everywhere—on car bumpers, stickers, bandanas, storefronts, and brandished in windows on standards and banners—the flag once again became the symbol of eternal America. Not long after, Arianne Phillips, stylist for Madonna, telephoned. The singer wanted a piece from Catherine's patriotic fashion show. Madonna, as flag bearer of the label, was all it took to inscribe Catherine Malandrino on the list of fashion designers who matter. She joined the ranks of designers whose low-cut necklines attract the lenses of the world's photographers who gather around the red carpet on Oscar night, and whose dresses sweep the stairs at the Cannes Film Festival. John Galliano telephoned Catherine. "I love it," he said. "I would like to wear a piece for the finale of my next haute couture show." The most famous of the designs, however, was to become the American flag wrap-dress. Halle Berry, Julia Roberts, and Sharon Stone were photographed on the covers of women's magazines wearing the cult dress, which was later displayed in Zandra Rhodes' Fashion and Textile Museum in London.

the first three years in America had proven quite a journey for Malandrino. And in fact, it was a chance meeting in 1997 that redirected the path of the young Frenchwoman. She was then designing the Et Vous collections in Paris. On a business trip to Manhattan, she met Bernard Aidan, subsidiary owner of the Et Vous label in the United States. "The man gave me wings," Catherine says today. The Algonquin Hotel, the symbolic site of 1920s bohemian New York as embodied by Dorothy Parker and her friends, provided the backdrop for their first meeting. The pair's connection was immediate. That same day Bernard and Catherine bought a piece of patchwork from Pennsylvania at a flea market on Twenty-third Street. They have kept it as a talisman. Catherine, hand in hand with her love, discovered New York in a new way, street by street, neighborhood by neighborhood. From then on, the two have walked together as liberated individuals who respect each other's independence and still today refuse the ties of marriage.

With Bernard at her side, Catherine moved stateside, and her career gained momentum. The first collection signed Catherine Malandrino was presented the same year in their downtown loft. At that time, and for the next four seasons, Catherine designed collections for Diane Von Furstenberg by day and draped her own models by night. One year after her son, Oscar, was born, her first fashion show, *Collage*, took place in New York in 1998. In an interview with Christina Ha for the television program *Behind the Label*, the designer said, "It was like I felt that I have something to express, a vision of a woman. The lifestyle is refined, but cool; the clothes are easy and amazingly shaped. And I knew that at a point, I had to express it on my own because I felt that I was the best one to express it, because I was feeling it so strongly [in] me."

"New York gave me a sense of power," says Catherine, who always links Bernard with her success. It was quite surprising, a Frenchwoman giving fashion shows on American soil. They were expecting her in Paris, and here she was in New York! "The first time I met [Catherine] was for her…show in Harlem. Nobody went to Harlem," exclaimed Dawn Mello, former president of Bergdorf Goodman and a fashion consultant, as she recalled the *Hallelujah* collection, shown in 2001. But Catherine had no hesitation. After all, just one year earlier she had quite audaciously cut patterns in the Stars and Stripes. Harlem, with its mix of races and cultures, fed her imagination and inspired her. She drew power from the women who donned their most beautiful adornments to sing their devotion in church and who covered their heads with flowered caps, hats, cotton ruffles, and three-penny lace. Catherine dared to abolish boundaries, presenting her collection in the famous Apollo Theater, where Duke Ellington and Count Basie had set the rhythm, and where others had followed, such as the Pointer Sisters and Prince. While still in Paris, Catherine had envisioned these blues voices as accompaniment for the show, appropriately presented on a Sunday at noon, when gospel fervor still vibrated in Harlem's churches. Model Lya opened the show in a cotton dress embroidered with huge white flowers. She was followed by the aristocratic Erin O'Connor nonchalantly wearing an Afro and a silk dress that resembled lingerie from the 1920s. Models marched onstage to Léopold Sédar Senghor:

> "I have seen Harlem humming with sounds and solemn color / And flamboyant smells… / I have seen night readying itself at the flight of day. / And I proclaim Night more truthful than Day" ("Ethiopiques" in *Poèmes*, Le Seuil, Paris, 1956).

Hidden behind her large black sunglasses, Catherine, the night butterfly, absorbed the energy of the neighborhood and the power of jazz. The *Hallelujah* fashion show was a melting pot of images and references, blond Afros, street urchin caps, bare feet, slashed skirts, and an ode to the city and to music. The designer was already showing her attraction to other cultures and to the cosmopolitan.
Travel and a mix of influences shape her work. This thirst for somewhere else is apparent in all her creations—from Russian tradition in handmade macramé to African culture in wood palette embroideries. From her trips to Thailand and Bali, Catherine would bring back images, virtual four-colored tourist pamphlets, to induce her to dream and to inspire her. Catherine is constantly on the move, traveling between Paris and New York, New York and Los Angeles, for inspiration and for pleasure. And so her collections always have a rhythm that belongs only to her, a quick tempo for dancing and rocking that brings together tradition and modernity in one musical score.

Her fashion follows the incessant beat of New York, the beat of the women she dresses—who also crisscross the planet—and the beat of the world.

Catherine feeds on her travels. She might escape to the Grand Canyon, cross it on a Harley Davidson and return with an idea, to create a parallel between the canyons of the West and the buildings of New York. Her *NY Canyon* collection, presented in 2002, included matte textures and cowboy boots ornamented with flowers. Lace and voile wool dresses recalled the skirted silhouettes of the cowgirls of the American West, albeit cowgirls with eyes darkly charcoaled. Catherine finds her inspiration in the world around her.

"Anytime, anywhere, anyone," Catherine says, preferring the conciseness of the English language to sum up her influences. The *Movement* collection of 2003, presented at the Boat Basin Café on Manhattan's Upper West Side, reflected this ethos and was radically more urban, with comfortable, soft volumes, ultrafeminine satin, and draped voile fabric with sporty overtones. It was the Parisian ballerina Marie-Claude Pietragalla dancing with a veil in the dreamy ballet *Raymonda*. Her next collection, *Slam Princess* (2003), was inspired by Russell Simmons' Broadway show *Def Poetry Jam*, in which slam poets performed their works live on stage. Just as the words chanted by the budding troubadours of a new culture were backed by music, Catherine's designs paraded the runway to a staccato hip-hop beat. Short dresses, fit and shapely, molded to the outlined silhouettes. The body became modeling clay at the service of the "look." The high-heeled boots and zipper trims perfectly highlighted the contours of the body. The energy of the urban black culture flowed by perfusion into our veins. Metal studs replaced embroidery, leather was paired with satin. Musician Lenny Kravitz was seduced and ordered from Catherine a leather motorcycle jacket covered with thirty-five hundred Swarovski crystal jewels in emerald, turquoise, ruby, and diamond colors. And it was not by chance that behind the scenes, the designer met the diva of R & B, the queen of hip-hop, born in the Bronx, Mary Jane Blige. There was a spark between the two women, the brunette and the peroxide blond, and Catherine would design many show gowns for the singer. Later, Mary J., on stage at the Zénith, in Paris, called out, "Catherine, I love you," an emotional moment for the two friends. Together, they shared Blige's summer 2007 tour, The Break Through Experience, and later that year, Mary J. Blige took the stage at the Roseland Ballroom during the presentation of Catherine's *Urban Queen* collection (Fall-Winter 2006), in which the models stood on a huge revolving platform. The "urban queen" introduced during this fashion show, this new queen of the city, as Catherine calls her, loves sensual fabrics, rich textures, the sheen of aged leather pants, the softness of a tulle jacket embroidered with white mink paired with the daintiness of a silk skirt. Other influences have similarly swayed collections. The *Night Owls* collection, presented in a Chelsea warehouse in 2004, was on the same wavelength as modern concerns about global warming and the planet's future. Science had asked the question, how do we become "thermo hybrid?" By mixing genres, answered Catherine Malandrino. Women, birds of the night, wore high-heeled sandals with large colorful socks made of cashmere; silk satin lingerie dresses embroidered with birds, were accessorized with Davy Crockett–style fur hats. The show advocated a return to natural materials and sources to save the planet. Catherine works solely with natural fibers, such as China silk, Swiss cottons, and Italian wools, and she explores the techniques and the knowledge of the craftsperson. A trip to Pennsylvania's Amish country inspired the designer's *Down to Earth* collection in 2006. "And be ye not conformed to this world," say the Anabaptists, who set themselves apart from modern culture and its emphasis on the individual. The fashion show was not a parade, but rather the creations were exhibited at the Pace Wildenstein gallery on models, like pillars of salt or works of art, and the public paraded. Clay and raw canvas colors, cotton lace, macramé and almost puritan flared forms were the themes for this return to the earth. The suit jacket held the place of honor in the collection, with its small shoulders, tiny bust, and cinched waist. Catherine cut one-of-a-kind strapless dresses and Amish frock coats from handmade cotton and linen patchworks. Embroidery with wooden shapes and beads enhanced crisp silk taffeta. The main accessories presented at the show were shoes designed as jewelry. Wood and metal soles, thick heels sculpted with flowers, and the association of macramé, leather, and rope created a cult accessory.

"To be irreplaceable, you have to be always different," said Gabrielle Chanel, whom Catherine freely quotes as an inspiring force. Catherine's designs take their references from the haute couture tradition. Catherine Malandrino learned the craft in the workshops of designers Emmanuel Ungaro and Louis Féraud. She molds fabric to the body in the style of Madeleine Vionnet, another woman whose work Catherine admires. Catherine reinvents the drapings, pleats, topstitching, and ribbing that make a design a unique piece. She handles scissors and sticks in pins, creating a personal relationship with the clothing. "I always try on my dresses to validate my ideas," she says. In her notepads she draws her small sketches like comic-strip sequences, with women in the forefront, in real-life situations, in movement.

Raised in a warm and feminine environment, Catherine fondly remembers her loving parents: an entrepreneurial father and a mother who projected her desire for independence and professional fulfillment on her four daughters. The relationships between Catherine, Anne, Hélène, and Elisabeth remain deep and close despite the distance. No matter where travels take them, not a week goes by that they don't talk. Catherine helps women find themselves in their femininity by expressing their most intimate and personal, and also their most triumphant, selves. Dressed in Malandrino, a woman becomes a queen herself. Catherine's mother says of her daughter, "Catherine has a dream and needs to transcend the ordinary to satisfy her imagination. As a child, she sketched dresses and then made them, creating her own fantastic world. She has an innate desire to realize her vision."

Hollywood understands this well, welcoming the Frenchwoman with open arms. Demi Moore dressed in Catherine Malandrino for the premiere of her screen comeback, in 2003; stars such as Jennifer Aniston, Elizabeth Hurley, Sarah Jessica Parker, and Charlize Theron give Catherine their trust. Another fan from the A-list, Heidi Klum, says, "Catherine's clothes are elegant, amusing, sensual, and wearable at the same time, always with a zest of difference. I like the care she gives to the details. In one of her dresses, I can go from a television set to a lunch, always elegant and with the feeling of being unique. Her fashion is multiple and fits my skin." But there is more to Malandrino's clients than just famous faces. "Beyond the celebrity," Catherine says, "there is always a meeting with a woman." She speaks of her first contact with Angelina Jolie, the Hollywood goddess and generous personality involved in many charitable causes. In a studded silk dress called Starburst, a Catherine Malandrino Limited Edition, the American actress posed for the cover of *Rolling Stone* magazine. Catherine also talks about Halle Berry, the sculptural actress. "She wanted to wear the Flag dress in silk muslin. Phillip Bloch, with whom I work, cut the sleeves—a deep Y-cut on her glowing, honey-colored skin," says Catherine. She mentions the musicians Les Nubians "for their spirits that come from far away."

f or these exceptional women and for all the others, Catherine designs pieces that can be appropriated by the wearer. "The pieces are not frozen. They have to live and have their own autonomy," she says. "A coat or a long sweater can be worn as a dress." Every item of clothing has its truth, and like in Pirandello's theater, every client interprets that truth for herself. Catherine happily recounts a few anecdotes on this subject: the story of a woman, trying on clothes in New York, who lifted the large collar of a sweater to wear it as a hood; or the noted arrival in a New York City restaurant of a client who had decided to wear a knitted skirt as a poncho. The initial surprise over, the stylist appreciates how others can "own" her inspiration, her designs. She appreciates it when an article of clothing linked to an important moment in someone's life merges with a memory. Her collections are divided into two parts—Malandrino and Catherine Malandrino—to meet that need for exclusivity and one-of-a-kind pieces.

Times have changed. In France, the Chanel woman, deprived of the right to vote, had everything to prove and left floating in her wake a trace of N°5 so that we would not forget her. Now a part of the world's onward march, the woman who dresses in Catherine Malandrino manages her life on her iPhone or BlackBerry. She may live in Manhattan or in Los Angeles. Like Catherine, she has gained financial independence by her own means, while remaining attached to her role as a mother, sister, and friend. Catherine's son, Oscar, who was born and raised in the fashion world (models would hold him after fittings or backstage at her fashion shows), is proudly part of his mom's success. And it is just for him that Catherine designs exclusive T-shirts and leather jackets studded with his name. In these many roles, Catherine is a leader, and one who need not be so on a man's terms. Rather she may take charge in an ultra-feminine dress with bouffant sleeves, perched on high heels. Why borrow from a masculine dressing room when feminine clothing can be so rich? In the designer's opinion, the desire to wear a broad-shouldered jacket, a pale imitation of a bodybuilder's silhouette, is simply the expression of a lack of self-confidence. Catherine explains her success in part by this break with the minimalist design of the '80s, this return to a feminine reality inspired by enigmatic heroines like Anouk Aimée in *8½*. The Frenchwoman is aware that in many areas equality is yet to be won, but with her typical mild determination and her unbeatable confidence—doubt is always inspirational for her—she reveals another path, her path, and vindicates us with her words. Catherine's woman is delicious, mysterious, sensual, and in love. "At heart, the dress" would become, in a way, the new slogan of an up-and-coming generation that to make an impact, would no longer need to resort to transvestism or borrowing the codes of the "other." The dress emphasizes emotion and sensitivity; it uncovers and expresses feelings. As Julien Clerc sang, *"La Belle Est Arrivée."* Catherine met the singer at a concert he gave in New York, and he became friends with her and Bernard. "The woman's in a dress, she's showing her legs," Catherine likes to say. It's no accident that performer Zizi Jeanmaire was the virtual godmother of the 2007 collection, and her world of feathers and spangles was the backdrop of the fashion show. "Her legs are longer than her body," said the writer Boris Vian of Jeanmaire. Catherine sought that same elongated silhouette by dressing her models in a single piece, wedding the body's curves. The flowing dress became timeless, the signature of the woman who wears it. It sang: "*Moi vouloir toi. De haut en bas*" ("I want you, from top to bottom"), like the singer Françoise Hardy did in the early 1980s. Catherine began with a low neckline, designed to form a sort of fabric necklace using ornamentation—a stitch, a mini pleat, pearl embroidery—to create a piece of clothing jewelry. Then came the soft shoulders, followed by ultrafeminine, transparent puffed sleeves. Smooth, rounded curves took the place of angles.

Catherine is a perfectionist who can, for example, spend a whole night redesigning an embroidery inspired by a mosaic from the Blue Mosque, which she saw during a trip to Istanbul. Cut in flowing fabrics—a muslin, a voile—the designs are always in movement. The driest materials such as wool crepe are retreated, washed, and softened to obtain a softer, silkier feel. Washed leather is reworked and becomes smooth, lustrous. The tightest weaves are made airy by geometric cutouts that against the skin create a peekaboo game of desire. A wrinkle crepe folded like origami, a slit-front panel on a fringed skirt lighten an outfit, deconstructing the structure. There is nothing rigid, nothing brittle. This is the search for harmony above all else. Zizi Jeanmaire and dancer Roland Petit, intertwined, dancing together onstage and in the city, in the image of Catherine and Bernard, sharing the same dream. Catherine remembers her days sprinkled with love notes on Post-its; e-mails exchanged with Bernard, whether he was on the floor above or in the room next door; fittings interrupted by a kiss. Echoing her personal story, the clothes murmur, suggest, and inspire rather than impose. The stylist cites Anouk Aimée in *A Man and a Woman* and Romy Schneider in *The Swimming Pool*, actresses who were all softness, but emotional and passionate as well. All this might well trigger the imagination, like characters in a novel lead the reader into new lands. The *La Coupole* collection, presented in 2005 at New York's Gotham Hall, was such a trigger and foreshadowed Catherine's return to Paris for the opening of the boutique on rue des Saint-Pères in winter 2006. Former husband and wife Serge Gainsbourg and Jane Birkin, new lovers of the Malandrino story, embodied this passion collection, which was also packed with references to Victorian-era lovers: embroidered tulle blouses, cropped, pleated jackets, shirtwaists with ruffled fronts worn with silk-taffeta jodhpur pants, fitted jackets in ribbed faille, and sweaters designed as blouses with bouffant sleeves and modest necklines. And what is more sensual than the netting with which Catherine Malandrino punctuates her collections: Oversize sweaters hide a thin body, but the mesh drapes on one shoulder, open-work fabric on a breast, exposes it. Here, the couture netting is open, reworked; it is enveloping, luxurious, and desirable.

The fabrics evoke desire and beckon the fingertips. And one has to touch, of course, but one also has to see. For Catherine, desire is also expressed through color, a call to love. In her design studio, Catherine keeps a wall of Polaroid images, chaotic photo collages of her family and friends—her son, Oscar, with

Dr. Michel Cohen; her friend Sélima, who designs eyeglasses; Stacey Kaye Bronfman, her first friend in New York; Véronique Gabai-Pinsky, her first SoHo client and still her loyal friend; and Freddie Leiba, who has accompanied her for the last three years at her fashion shows. Images and colors of those she loves surround her.

t he 1990s had brought the beginning of startups and the infancy of the Internet in a unipolar world. After the fall of the Berlin Wall, America was the only great power in contention. Progress was measured in the cloning of Dolly the sheep. Fashion's elegant "uniform," its version of cloning, became the new proposal for the workingwomen who pushed their way into the glass towers and clicked their heels in the ascending elevators as the doors closed noiselessly on belted silhouettes. Catherine, glossing her sketchbooks with clean paint colors, vibrated with excitement at the Pantone colors of pop art, the prints by Roy Lichtenstein and the *Big Splash* by David Hockney.

In fashion, color awakens the fabric. Thus, yellow, the "color of the sun, of lemon," is the signature color of the label. "It's an urban yellow, edgy, associated with the light of the city," says Catherine. Her colors are never powdered, faded, or diluted. She displays clear, primary, even ardent tonalities on the walls of her home and in the snapshots of her fashion shows. At the end of the 1990s, the arrival in black-and-white New York of a chromatic collection in shades of lemon with touches of pink—the color of bougainvillea—and fern green warmed the spirits in an otherwise gray world of fashion. Colors served as a backdrop for her creations then and still do today. It is not mere happenstance that an ordinary object, a package of Gitanes forgotten on a zinc bar, inspired her Gitane clutch, in shades of blue, in the *Smoking or Not-Smoking* collection presented with stylist Lori Goldstein in 2004. (Goldstein had chosen the *Flag* collection to illustrate the cover of Italian *Vogue*, giving Catherine one of her first press covers with model Gisèle Bündchen and photographer Steven Meisel.) Like the artists of the '50s who found their inspiration in ordinary objects such as comic strips, Catherine drew upon the Gitane package's famous silhouette of a tambourine dancer masked by smoke spirals, drawn by Mollusons and Max Ponty and retouched by others. The Gitane, "inspiration" for artists such as Serge Gainsbourg, became the muse for a fashion show. Gitane blue fit perfectly in the Malandrino spectrum, soft without being pastel. The gossamer, voluptuous dresses, in silk muslin, evoked the refound freedom.

Other colors and other references developed. An earthy ochre brown was dominant in the natural looks of the Amish-inspired *Down to Earth* collection of 2006. There were also some twenty shades of purples, gradients from pink to fuchsia, from sky blue to turquoise, these intense tones more dramatic than romantic. Catherine, with her pale white skin and black hair, is her own primary model. Her beauty enhances both the acidy shades and the warm tones of color present in her designs—or is it the other way around? For her, color essentially acts as a revealer, as writing on the skin. It is a story of melanin and an invitation to desire. The designs that Catherine draws are eminently sensual. In this sense, also, they speak a universal and contemporary language. The woman is "comfortable in her skin," fully inhabiting her corporal envelope; better still, she shows it, and she knows how to play with it. The *Down to Earth* collection had a sensual, down-to-earth side, perfectly illustrated by the diamond-shaped cotton lace insets and by the slashes cut in the sleeves, which revealed a tiny bit of skin, like snowflakes cut in folded paper— those naïve designs that when spread out flat, create a surprise.

I t is impossible to separate design from the world. "Fashion is not only a story about clothes, it is carried by the wind. We feel it, in the sky, on the road," Catherine remarks. As a Jack Kerouac of fashion, she follows her own path in the city. She has settled with her family beside the Hudson River. She thinks about the Seine, and about her nomadic life in a new century, dividing her life and finding her inspiration between the two continents. Her loft reflects her unquestionable taste and an interior harmony toward which she leans at every moment. Inside, we find primary variations of yellow and red—on the walls and on the furniture, which includes a scarlet sofa signed Piero Lissoni for Cappellini, the orange of the famous plastic Dax chair by Charles and Ray Eames, and of the ribbon chair by Pierre Paulin. Color dominates the objects—her collections of Murano glass, her Reed and Barton enamel and silver bowls. It lives in the '50s and '60s furniture design—a glass table by Eileen Gray, a vintage globe lamp found in a flea market, a modular silver candleholder by Nagel. It vibrates in the artwork—Russian propaganda posters from the 1930s, the works of contemporary New York artists such as Kareem Iliya and Jeannie Weissglass. Catherine finds her references, her vocabulary, and she also uses it at home and in her stores. The first retail space was in SoHo. It was 1998. The neighborhood was completely changing. While awaiting the new millennium, the '80s were laid to rest there. Andy Warhol had immortalized his contemporaries in colored silkscreen prints, and

Jean-Michel Basquiat had indelibly graffitied on our memories his drawings of wounded children. Catherine Malandrino and Bernard Aidan would make a stop in this emerging place. The citrus walls of the Broome Street store formed a sharp contrast with the monolithic New York of the period, whose fashion was a checkerboard in black-and-white programmed by two exclusive players, Donna Karan and Calvin Klein. Ahead of her time, Catherine Malandrino launched the vintage look, thinking of the store as a salon and decorating it with pieces by Anne Jacobsen and Eames, illustrations by her friend IZAK, lamps by Joe Colombo, and silk screen prints from *Derrière le miroir*, an art magazine published by the Maeght Foundation in Saint-Paul de Vence, a reference site for the designer. After the golden boys of the early '90s and before the super-rich of the new millenium, in this New York—in divorce proceedings with the underground— the Malandrino store was a curiosity, a haven of liberty and of joy for life, a friendly living room in which one listened to Gainsbourg, the French singer Barbara, or Claude Nougaro. It was the first lifestyle boutique in New York and was featured on the cover of the Italian *Elle Decoration* in 2000. Soon SoHo would come out of its cocoon, choose its place on the map, and become a neighborhood of fashion and design. Already the heroines of *Sex and the City* were arriving, like twenty-first century versions of the French comic book character *Pravda la survireuse*, the pride of Guy Peellaert. Wearing high heels, the red-haired Patricia Field, leader of the nocturnal world of transvestites, key figure of the 1980s and costume designer for *Sex and the City*, rushed to the store. A few weeks later Sarah Jessica Parker's Carrie Bradshaw shopped in the store for the already cult series, in an episode aired in 2002. It was a television moment that the fashionista would not forget! The day after the episode aired, a line in front of the store blocked the sidewalk. It was time to emigrate further to another evolving area, the Meatpacking District, where Catherine and Bernard, with their pioneer instinct, set up shop at the corner of Thirteenth Street, amidst hangars and warehouses.

nterior designer Christophe Pillet, a childhood friend, was the accomplice who executed the spaces. "We designed all the stores together: cement enclosures, tinted mirrors, colors of moss and green, or else amber shades," says the architect, who is an integral part of the architecture of the city itself for his screeching metal designs and his own glass house. But the design of the new Meatpacking District store borrowed from other imaginations, this time curved: the almost feminine contour of a sofa, the hyperboloid structures of Oscar Niemeyer, the eight hundred glass droplets in the Murano "Summer Rain" chandelier. The opening was based on Peter Sellers' film *The Party*, a comedy of errors from 1968, and was chosen as the occasion to present Catherine's first eponymous collection. Catherine drew on the strong relationships with her friends for the event. Isabella Rossellini's daughter Elettra, Lydia Hearst, and Theodora Richards modeled. The dresses were suspended by passementerie straps and by coral beads created by friend Harumi Klossowski. The models who danced to the sound of gypsy violins reminded one of Fellini heroines. After all, the collection was all Hollywood: silk caftans embroidered with silver or gold thread, passementerie pompom clusters, embroidered straw, and appliquéd flowers on Eton jackets. In each design could be seen the hand of the craftsperson, as well as the thread and the stitch. Catherine loves to laugh, to have fun, to live. Her lively and unique creations are tinged with humor. The search for individuality is at the heart of Catherine's work. In the same way, every store is a different space, designed as a walkway, a promenade—modular and free—implemented according to Catherine's desires and put into perspective by Christophe Pillet. The purpose is "to create spaces where each dress is encountered as a curiosity to make women dream," Catherine says. In years to come, there would be boutiques in Las Vegas, Miami, Moscow, Tokyo, and London. And as the stores evolved, so did the collections. On September 4, 2006, this time at the Roseland Ballroom, the 2007 *Metropolis* collection made reference to the future depicted in *Blade Runner*. But Catherine's gaze was riveted on a promising and positive future, marked by the planned opening of new spaces in emerging countries such as China, Dubai, India, Kuwait, Russia, and Turkey.

a s a designer, Catherine Malandrino's senses are all awakened. In an eponymous collection for Spring-Summer 2008, an orange satin dress with short spiral-flounced sleeves brings to mind a tangerine, the crumpling of silk, and the luminosity of the sun. For the design of a twenty-two-suite hotel in a palace in the heart of Florence, she is already thinking about the spectrum of colors, the textures, the perfume of the place, the intoxicating library, the images, and the paintings by contemporary artists that she imagines already hang in place. For her second store in Los Angeles, a cube of luminescent cement on Melrose Place, she thought about taste and envisioned a champagne bar and café. Her creativity expresses itself in many ways, in a line of ballerina flats designed for Repetto or a collection of jewelry that mixes solid silver, ceramic, and enamel. Spanning two cultures, two countries, she combines, matches, tears apart, and renews the associations in her mind to create a world that she imagines brought together all in one house, the female territory par excellence. One might visualize this place as halfway between the past and the future, between Old Europe and the New World, a place that would borrow from Pierre Chareau's glass house and the Maeght Foundation's contemporary, natural aesthetic. "Instead of talking about Catherine as a Parisian or a New Yorker, I would like to think of her as an international citizen because of her unique ability to please women around the world," says Dawn Mello. In Paris, she is called the New Yorker. In New York, they say she is so Parisian. But the multifaceted woman that Catherine imagines has no borders. She wears clothes that speak a universal language, the language of desire and of love.

ESCATE    COW BOY BOOTS    FALL 2002    Catherine Malandrino

*Spring / Summer Collection 2002*

# CATHERINE
# MALANDRINO

★ **HALLELUJAH!** ☆

★ **THE APOLLO THEATER**
253 WEST 125TH STREET, NEW YORK, NY

**SUNDAY, SEPTEMBER 9, 2001**

# SHOWTIME: 12 NOON

SECTION: _____    ROW: _____    SEAT: _____

Dress suspended
on a cutout satin
embroidery V neck

Silk georgette
+
crinkle silk chiffon

shirring for full
circle skirt
3 layers

"Easy rider"
'69

flag dress
silk crinkle
chiffon 3 layers

distress flag

extra
long shirt
dress

skirt in full
circle + pleated
pleats

masculine
construction
and detail

MALAN

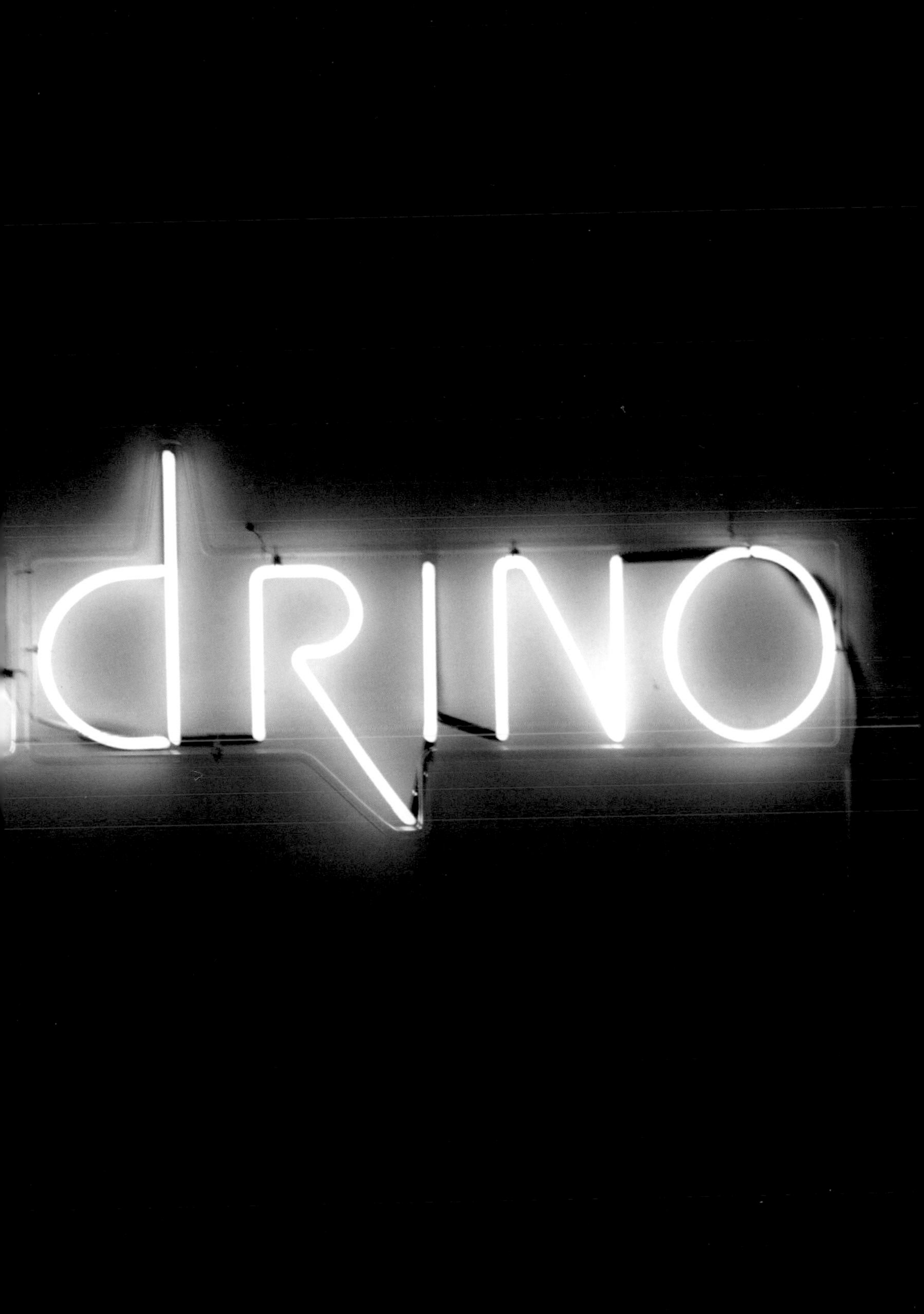
dRINO

FALL 2002 Catherine Malahdrino.

# Chronology

**1997:** Arrives in New York and meets Bernard Aidan, who becomes her professional and personal partner.

**1998:** Her son, Oscar, is born.
The first CATHERINE MALANDRINO boutique opens in SoHo at the corner of Broome and Greene Streets, with the aid of interior designer and childhood friend Christophe Pillet.

**2001:** The *Flag* collection, inspired by the American flag, debuts and is honored by the press. Madonna wears a piece from the collection onstage. After the events of September 11, the *Flag* collection develops a cult following and is adopted by stars such as Halle Berry, Julia Roberts, and Sharon Stone.
At the Apollo Theater in Harlem, Catherine Malandrino presents the *Halellujah* collection (Spring-Summer 2002) and meets the R & B singer Mary J. Blige, for whom she creates show gowns. The two develop a special friendship.

**2002:** An episode of the cult series *Sex and the City* is filmed in the CATHERINE MALANDRINO boutique in SoHo. The show's star, Sarah Jessica Parker, adores Catherine's collections. Her success extends out of New York and to the West Coast.

**2003:** Zandra Rhodes' Fashion and Textile Museum displays the now-famous Flag dress in London.
Following the *Slam Princess* fashion show (Fall-Winter 2003), Catherine Malandrino dresses Demi Moore for the premiere of her screen comeback in *Charlie's Angels*.

**2004:** Opens a second space in New York in the Meatpacking District and three more U. S. stores follow—in Manhasset, East Hampton, and Los Angeles.

**2005:** Makes a distinction between her two lines: MALANDRINO, a designer collection, and CATHERINE MALANDRINO, a contemporary collection.
Presents the *La Coupole* collection (Fall-Winter 2005) in Dubai.

**2006:** Opens her first Parisian boutique in Saint-Germain-des-Près.
Designs an exclusive collection for Repetto and creates bags and shoes for the MALANDRINO line.
Serves on the panel of judges in Paris and New York for the television show *Project Runway*.

**2007:** Presents the *Zizi* collection for Fall-Winter 2007 and the *La Colombe* collection for Spring-Summer 2008.
Charlize Theron wears Malandrino's mirror dress.
Presents the *Zizi* collection in Athens.
Holds her first fashion show in Moscow where she inaugurates a new MALANDRINO boutique in TSUM department store.

**2008:** Presents her first jewelry collection.
Opens her flagship store on Melrose Place in Los Angeles and a boutique in The Shoppes at the Palazzo in Las Vegas.
Plans international expansion with stores in Dubai, Istanbul, Kuwait, and Tokyo.

# CATHERINE MALANDRINO

Catherine Malandrino wearing her Flag dress from the *Flag* collection (Fall-Winter 2001) in front of her store in Manhatttan's Meatpacking District.
© Andrew Dosunmu.

Dennis Hopper's film *Easy Rider* (1969) was the inspiration for the *Flag* collection (Fall-Winter 2001). Shown from left: Dennis Hopper (as Billy) and Peter Fonda (as Wyatt). Courtesy of Silver Screen Collection; © 2006 Getty Images.

Still from the short film *Une Journée avec Catherine Malandrino*, directed by Andrew Dosunmu. © Andrew Dosunmu.

Model Chrystèle Saint Louis Augustin walks the runway for the *Flag* collection (Fall-Winter 2001) in body paint. Photo courtesy Catherine Malandrino.
A handmade cashmere baseball jacket and silk chiffon skirt from the *Flag* collection. Photo courtesy Catherine Malandrino.

Delfine Bafort models for the *NY Canyon* collection (Fall-Winter 2002). Photo courtesy Catherine Malandrino.
Catherine poses on a New York street wearing a piece from her *NY Canyon* collection. Photo from personal archives.

Catherine's sketch of cowboy boots from the *NY Canyon* collection (Fall-Winter 2002). Photo courtesy Catherine Malandrino.
Model Carolina B. wears a silk jersey devoré dress (*NY Canyon*) in a photo shoot for Le Bon Marché in 2002. © Wendelien Daan.

The Apollo Theater in Harlem, where Catherine Malandrino presented her *Hallelujah* collection (Spring-Summer 2002).
© John Van Hasselt/CORBIS SYGMA.
An invitation to the Spring-Summer 2002 show for the *Hallelujah* collection.

**The finale** of the *Hallelujah* fashion show at the Apollo Theater (Spring-Summer 2002). Photo courtesy Catherine Malandrino.

**Model Carolina B.** strikes a dramatic pose in a limited-edition Swarovski crystal-studded leather jacket from the *Slam Princess* collection.
© Wendelien Daan.

**Mary J. Blige, Odile Gilbert, Alek Wek, and Catherine Malandrino** smile backstage at the show for *Urban Queen* (Fall-Winter 2006). Photo courtesy Catherine Malandrino.

**Models** stand on a revolving podium during the *Urban Queen* show (Fall-Winter 2006). Photo courtesy Catherine Malandrino.

**A sandal** from the *Metropolis* accessories collection (Spring-Summer 2007). © Tom Munro.
**Model Mina Cvetkovic** wearing the solar dress in duchess satin from the *Metropolis* collection (Spring-Summer 2007). © Tom Munro.

**Catherine Malandrino** sketching a new collection. Photo courtesy Catherine Malandrino.
**A page** from her sketch book. Photo courtesy Catherine Malandrino.

*Metropolis* collection (Spring-Summer 2007). The models stand on metal scaffolding reminiscent of the architecture of New York City. Photo courtesy Catherine Malandrino.

**The neon Malandrino sign** from the *Metropolis* fashion show (Spring-Summer 2007). Photo courtesy Catherine Malandrino.

**Snapshots from backstage** at the *Metropolis* fashion show (Spring-Summer 2007). © Roxanne Lowit.
**Bernard Aidan** and Catherine Malandrino. Photo from personal archives.

**The custom-made "Summer Rain" chandelier** at the Meatpacking District store in New York showcases eight hundred Murano glass droplets. © Bärbel Miebach.

**Early morning at Café de Flore** on Saint-Germain-des-Prés in Paris. © Jean-Loup Sieff.
**A clutch** from the *Smoking or Not-Smoking* collection (Spring-Summer 2005), an homage to the smoke-inspired logo of the French cigarette brand Gitanes. Photo courtesy Catherine Malandrino.

**A fitting session** before the show for the *La Colombe* collection (Spring-Summer 2008). © Wendelien Daan.
**Work in progress.** © Thomas Nicol.

**A sketch** by Catherine Malandrino. Photo courtesy Catherine Malandrino.
**Model Andressa** wears the silk Flower bolero and Promenade trousers from the *La Colombe* collection (Spring-Summer 2008). © Wendelien Daan.

**A stiletto** from the *Metropolis* accessories collection (Spring-Summer 2007). © Tom Munro.
**Model Judith Bedard** wears the wool scallop Night gown and embroidered Macadam leather jacket with a silver-and-green necklace in the style of Templier, from the *Greenhouse* collection (Fall-Winter 2008). © Wendelien Daan.

Models **Coco Rocha** and **Carolina Trentini** at the show for the *La Colombe* collection (Spring-Summer 2008). Photomontage by Thomas Nicol.
**A street** in Saint-Paul de Vence, France. © Guillaume Laurent.

**Model Andressa** captures the fluid motion of the silk jersey Bird dress from the *La Colombe* collection (Spring-Summer 2008). © Wendelien Daan.
**Model Atong** jumps skyward in the organza print Aragon dress from the *La Colombe* collection (Spring-Summer 2008). © Wendelien Daan.

**Model Judith Bedard** in the Petrol silk jersey dress with pleat detail and draped sleeves; multicolored jewel Parade necklace from the *Greenhouse* collection (Fall-Winter 2008). © Wendelien Daan.
**New York Harbor's iconic Statue of Liberty,** or, as Catherine calls her, "Lady Libertine." Photo by Margaret Bourke-White. © Getty Images.

**At left, a deep V cut** adds drama to the green satin duchess Fleur dress. At right, the emerald green and blue Colvert gown features stained-glass–like embellishment. Both dresses modeled by Judith Bedard. © Wendelien Daan.

# Acknowledgments

The publisher wishes to thank the following for their help and their invaluable contributions to this book:

Catherine Malandrino and Bernard Aidan, Pascale Richard, and Stéphanie Labeille-Sczyrba, as well as Celine Danhier, Celine Mariton, Thomas Nicol, Béatrice Dupire, Julie de Noailles, Véronique Gabai-Pinsky, and Angélique Dorier.

Special thanks to Mary J. Blige.

Much appreciation is also due to: Andressa, Atong, Carolina B., Delfine Bafort, Judith Bedard, Barbara Berger, Phillip Bloch, Luc Alexis Chasleries, Mina Cvetkovic, Wendelien Daan, Andrew Dosunmu, Nancy Dunham, Alyson Dusseault, Marilyn Gaultier, Odile Gilbert, Freddie Leiba, Dilcia Johnson, Lori Goldstein, Frederick Kennedy, Guillaume Laurent, Roxanne Lowit, Bärbel Miebach, Ryan Molloy, Yannick Morisot, Tom Munro, Jean Claude MVODO, Christophe Pillet, Cathy Quinn, Coco Rocha, Chrystèle Saint Louis Augustin, Barbara Sieff, Carolina Trentini, John Van Hasselt, and Alek Wek.

With thanks to Valérie Tougard and Kay Guttmann at Éditions Assouline and Rebecca Behan, Miriam Hiersteiner, and Esther Kremer.